HAIRDO
Rachel B. Glaser

The Song Cave

Published by The Song Cave
www.the-song-cave.com
© 2017 Rachel B. Glaser
Design and layout by Mary Austin Speaker
Cover image by Ryan MacDonald

ISBN: 978-0-9967786-6-4
Library of Congress Control Number: 2016962694

FIRST EDITION

for JT and the Monday poem gang

TABLE OF CONTENTS

I AM AN ORCHID

which means I can die at any moment

I'm the most graceful thing in the grocery store
I have several beautiful heads
all the body parts
and people hunt me

I'm attached to a rod with a hair clip

love me and don't fear me
take me from the supermarket
make me the fanciest part of your lame living room

show everyone you're responsible
that you have a lover
a tall feminine plant

fuck me when no one's looking
if my manual tells you to
if we are both high on plant food
if your girlfriend's on her period

I know the Creator and the future
I am like the mean queen in a movie
but also the only beauty left in the world

WHEN BOYS SEE MOVIES ALONE

when boys see movies alone, they become men
by the closing credits
which wash over them like meaningful rain

a girl becomes a woman
when she edits her resume with a cruel attitude
when she wounds the dragon
during the solstice she does not believe in

a man becomes a woman during exciting, torturous months
in the privacy of his cabin

I knew a boy who became a beast before he could become a man
and a girl who became a puddle and then a horse
and then a serious dog and then a baby with womanly ways
and then a woman

WITH NO DESIRE TO CALL ANYONE I REACH FOR MY PHONE

somewhat moved in the temple
during my public speaking class
after the fireworks
I reach for my phone

"truly interesting" I say to your story at lunch
but I'm feeling for my phone's smooth screen
in each of my four pockets

I pick up a jacket and can tell from the weight
in fabric it makes a boxy shape

it isn't fancy
it's like a dumb boyfriend
a short diary
a live battery

it gives me a little batch of pleasure
calls out like a pet in a hiding spot

I see my phone and see myself

it vibrates my hand at the lecture
sits nicely at dinner

I put the phone on silent
so no one will wake me
then stare at the screen
waiting for someone to call

when I put it to my face
my face ends calls
my face links calls
the cover-up from my face rubs onto my screen
like its wearing cover-up on its face
like a silly lover
a dirty mirror

I am closer with the phone than the people in the phone
what disappointment when it slips underneath the driver's seat

I feel something for the raised name of my credit card
the authority of keys
but nothing like with the phone

each time I drop it it dimples like a rock

there is an electrical bond between us
it must be coated in germs

a sad bolt of freedom when I power it down
on the plane
when they force me

TWO DISCARDED LOVERS

two discarded lovers
of dull manboy McOwerts
live in the same room
for a number of years

McOwerts is elsewhere
picking his NCAA bracket

the discarded lovers are so familiar
with each other's faces
that if given god's magic editing pen
could easily alter the flaws
(Jennifer's small chin)
(Ruby's seesaw tooth)

McOwerts late night chats the closed windows
of his discarded lovers
Love me, he tells his Lacie Harddrive
Love is all, he tells his empty Dasani water
Remember love? to his wheel of packing tape

I hated you so much that the hate diamonded over into love,
Ruby tells Jennifer
Jennifer is searching for an old Amtrak ticket stub
that once meant the world to her

Look, McOwerts is chatting us even though we're invisible,
Ruby says

McOwerts makes a long playlist in Grooveshark
before his wifi takes a break and stays broken
Life is hell, he tells the empty cartridges of his printer
My health is bad, he tells his digital photoframe
Go Huskies, he says with little heart to his online bracket

It's as if I've been given too small a role in my own life,
Ruby confides to Jennifer
I want to go hiking, but only if someone dresses me and
forces me to, she says unhelpfully

Jennifer reaches for a cheap plastic animal under the bed
she exists on vitamins and leftovers

Remember Adrian? Ruby asks
I remember nothing before McOwerts, Jennifer says
but all Ruby hears is a sort of hiccupping

UNDER THE SOFT FOAM OF THE MOON

in my locked car
on my dead phone
I noodle for the stranger
inside the house, my family sleeps
everyone I love is asleep
but I'm looking at the thin hands of the bushes
noodling along
feeling moony
just barely charming a stranger
distracting him from the old cure of sleep
feeling Shakespearian
because the sky looks painted
and my voice is delivering
I'm carving a hideout in the stranger
homing up to him
walking the dark path between us
seeing my face in things that don't have my face
I can feel the sleep of my aging neighbors
the luxurious seclusion
the sky isn't black or grey
it's that good fur
that far fabric
of soft light
and my voice rings its recurring realizations
with dawdling human flair

a pretend music
to touch the stranger
strangers are half symbol half animal
and this one breaks in air
as I enter the night breathing
with the assured heart of a trespasser
filled with the lonely lives of dogs
curdled excess charm
and a childless levity
I walk like an ancient camera is tracking me
is still interested when I bore myself
a night camera set to record the moon

DEODORANTS GROW BORED OF THEIR SMELL

they breathe it in and can't think of anything else
an Unscented one takes on a metallic scent
they overwhelm themselves and want to run out
but last forever and slowly lose their minds

9

IT IS ILLEGAL TO LIKE YOU

I am a hermit glued in a castle
and you, a former Taliban photographer
studying bullshit abroad

I must be the daughter of someone important
because I wear a headdress
I languish and parts of me die
on hold for Quest Diagnostics

I listen to your heart and hear nature's fucked clock
I read you easily like a book with a low reading level
or baby Suess's scribbled journal

you look like a meter with the coin stuck in the slot
you slip through my fingers like sand from a souvenir

random habits you've picked up and kept
sit inside you like strangers on a bus

behold your future, that thing obstructing the sun
and your past, a tedious board game played as punishment

I receive you resolutely
the way I carry recycling out

I take your hand
like a squid missing from the aquarium

your disdain is Disdain 101
a class I placed out of in high school

your tears are worth something
they make my thighs feel like swan meat
and thunder

I requill my own sex-history into striped bed sheets
a teenaged sticky thinking
I tell the story of the Jews
to a distracted hanger-on

when I was small I met my dark side under a lake
I wrote your name in the snow with my Ouija shoe
I heard your hair in the night

but now
your eyes benign heat seekers
the day, a discount ribbon

I ruin my fingers and decent pre-childbirth body
paraphrasing another woman's manifesto
while my ferret eats through my cords

the tree looked like an old wizard dying at an art museum
wake up and be him
I demanded of you
wrap your robes tightly
curse the sand in your lenses

remember me like the doll you had
before your Dad beheaded it

TEENAGE GIRLS HOT FOR THE EIFFEL TOWER

teenage girls hot for the Eiffel Tower
frame old French illustrations of cats
endure the death smell of nail polish
and create a self-religion in the shower
they only excel at field hockey
if they pretend they are fighting for France
their postcard idea of France
their ruffled dream of sex
these girls use the little lock on their doors
though their parents never bother them
though no boys ever call on the phone
they want to have the longest hair of anyone at school
but Therese will always have the longest hair
they have this idea of what whiskey will taste like
but the taste is really more like pralines
they want a boy to watch them cry
they want a hand mirror to examine their sex parts
they want a man to cross the coffee shop where they sit
and ask them what they're writing

CAN YOU FIND ME?

I'm in my parents' house
where part of me remains
I'm on white sheets
for real
I am
my finger smells like the most dangerous perfume
I'm nude as a painting
did you know I'm addicted to email?
I am
I once bought a taxidermied frog on eBay
it was dressed like a policeman
I gave it to my first boyfriend
where's it now?
somewhere among the chaos
ground into bits
last night I flirted with a dude
by giving him my social security number
have you ever tried that?
my hair is so unkempt that I just felt like Kurt Cobain
as I stepped over the yoga mat
and checked out my boobs in the mirror
John is in Silentland with the teen monks
do you know John?
he is the sweetest
his neck is a place

he's got great hair
he almost never channels Kurt Cobain
he's more like Harpo
or Olive Oyl
I had to Google the spelling of that
do you ask your most embarrassing questions
on Incognito tabs in Chrome?
I do
I ask about love and read the message boards
I love reading frantic wtf messages
from women about to be married
I like the desperation
and the frankness
I like when the original poster returns to the board to update us
I like being part of "us"
I'm wearing my mouth guard now
can you hear the difference?
a naked woman talking like a little girl
is like something you see in a circus
in the natural circus
like a mother with food on her nose
or two catfish quietly in love

THOSE WOMAN WOMAN MAN THREESOMES IN PORN

look like a group homework assignment
goofing off in someone's house
one person doing something that looks like work
but is really pretty easy
like one woman is just braiding the hair
of the woman being penetrated
or two women are licking the man's dick in a way
that would take centuries for him to come
they lose themselves in work
like astronauts
they see a mouth and kiss it
Jesse's pubes end up on their tongue
they've never seen nipples like Korinne's
they forget if Anne came
I touch the dick like it's all dicks
I've got an appointment at the vet
but Korinne makes me forget
she's tired and touching boobs only
Jesse is paralyzed by indecision
I whisper to him
from my place near his crotch
take Korinne from behind
and I'll crawl over there and kiss her
or just lay beneath her and be kissed

GUYS WEARING SUITS IN ACTION MOVIES
(THE ENEMY'S FRIENDS)

they laugh and look menacing
they trot around pools
sometimes they're eating sandwiches when they're shot

the enemy was mean to his friends and it made them mean
he was gruff and it made them gruff

sometimes when they are eating sandwiches the enemy scolds them
they need to protect the enemy!
or the mansion!
or go get the money!

the guys have guns (black or silver)
they bleed in their suits
they live to die

decorative plates are shot off the mantel
as the enemy flees the dining room
slipping on Spanish tiles

his dogs bark enthusiastically
a bullet nails him to the wall

he makes one last joke
and dies resenting his friends

they weren't his *real* friends
they were only drawn to his power
sometimes they didn't leave the bathroom as clean as they found it
they never did normal guy things
they were always wearing suits

WHERE'S MY WHIMSY?

I had so much whimsy
I had too much whimsy
ask my lovers
I was light
I lit up at strangers' dogs
and funny names
there was confetti
it was always my birthday
my hair curled with glee
I twisted with happiness
in the backseat of cabs
on the futons of friends

any despair gave the whimsy a break
I even liked the despair
I could get into the despair

at Kinko's I pressed the hot paper to my chest
friends called in despair and I lent them whimsy

over time, despair mixed with whimsy
and canceled out like numbers
there was a cool balance
my objects knew me as Her

there was a distance
a grim Mona Lisa smile

I can see the whimsy trapped in a girl's ring
I saw it in a photo shoot on the train tracks
I have an eye for it
I can summon it at Bat Mitzvahs
I'm not a stranger to it
but once it tittled out of me
I dispensed it like candies
it carnivaled around

I MISS MY ENEMY

and the desperation during parties
the elastic whip of emotion
battering the sidewalk
I want a girl to look at me with disdain
while I pull her boyfriend away from her
like an Arab scarf from a fire
I want to lie on the Persian rug
while my phone convulses from long distance calls
I stroke the face of my European boyfriend
I yank off his Brazilian soccer jersey
"Get real," my enemy hisses from the keyhole
I pause, a real Arian pause
"I'm so real," I say
and unbraid all the braids in my hair
nothing unnerves me
my enemy saunters in
and I watch her pleased
my phone drones on with rings
from unknown numbers
the boy hesitates
"Don't hesitate, Albert,"
she says, "we find it very unattractive"

TRAGIC SNOOPYS

shriveled Snoopy
bent or dented Snoopy
burnt Snoopys
deflated Snoopys
shredded Snoopys
grilled Snoopy
stained Snoopys
shards of Snoopy in the street
rusted Snoopy
oily Snoopys at the bottom of the barrel
cracked and leaking Snoopy
the boiled Snoopy I saw in Russia
diced Bulgarian Snoopy
the corroded Snoopy on 8th st.
matted
lumpy
coma Snoopy
scratched or bleeding Snoopy
Siamese Snoopys
hugely fat Snoopy
stick-thin Snoopy
the bratty imposter Snoopy
scorned half-made Snoopys
poopy Snoopy
pile-of-Snoopy

the dried eyes of Snoopy under glass
cheap Snoopy imitation on the television
Snoopy fossils sold instead of studied
a dazed half-alive Snoopy
with the tread worn off
with the light gone out
the heart not in
a clicking sound
a wind-up tail
puffy CGI Snoopy
nuclear glow Snoopy
pimped out Snoopy
and this is not Snoopy at all
Snoopy doesn't have a bell
or any fins
that is not Snoopy's coiled hair
Snoopy's metal screw
the flag is not from Snoopy
the shoe doesn't fit Snoopy
look, it's the Snoopy from your high school
condemned Snoopy
illegal Snoopy dripping in the church basement
Snoopy slime scrubbed from the retaining wall
shellacked Snoopy on the walking bridge
twisted Snoopy in the turbine
I remember the last Snoopy in the marsh
and the one we passed in the car
a hawk carrying Snoopy into the sky

RESPECT

I respected my brother when
growing up, he ordered oil & vinegar for his salad
and they brought him a metal contraption
that held two beakers for Einstein
like the scales of justice
yellow oil
and an insane purple

GUITAR TEACHER

the girl loves the guitar teacher
but loves everything that summer

but especially the guitar teacher
who teaches in music stores
in basements
in the grass like a god
or someone who's seen god

guitar teachers don't have good clothes
their heroes stare from album covers
while the guitar teachers sigh and strum
and summon youth

the notes
there is something clear in the notes

the girl makes the guitar teacher feel old
but occasionally legendary
she holds her music book
she wants to learn a Doors song and he laughs
the song is all bass
but he figures it out for her
remembering a dream he had
just the night before

he was dancing with the girl
while a boy watched them
burning
a boy that didn't play guitar
or have a voice
at least not a singing voice

eventually the guitar teacher backed away
and let the boy try to dance
the girl was in the very highlight of her life
like a sea creature shimmering in the sun
the guitar teacher has been tracking this light
this growing understanding of her own freedom
inside and outside a guitar solo
the wandering song
that long ago led the guitar teacher out of his parents' house
and into the exciting, gritty parts of town
into the arms of girls who liked the Doors
liked Jim Morrison
though no guitar teacher really loves Jim Morrison
no good guitar teacher

the girl isn't that different than those girls
has the same wild laugh
has taken the idea of a hippie and ran with it
with scarfs and lamps
and the poems of Charles Bukowski
the guitar teacher wants to show the girl sex

how it was shown to him
but she is dancing with the boy
and her light is blinding

WHILE I WAS A TREMENDOUS TEENAGER, YOU WERE STILL READING THE UNAUTHORIZED BIOGRAPHY OF BOWSER

you were holding a pube to the light
you were pressing your silly putty back in its egg
I was already part of an art movement
when you were asking when your birthday was
you were attempting to sing a jingle
you were tasting your bath water
I had the gall to put all my money on black
while you were talking softly to your toys
and asking the World Book about sex
I was gunning down the highway
while they shot my documentary
you were forking peas all afternoon
mulling over a bubble in your wallpaper
nervously saving your allowance
playing Rock Paper Scissors by yourself
I couldn't be bothered to read my fan mail
you were choosing a middle name for your rabbit
you were digesting yesterday's strudel
pretending tic-tacs were illegal
putting your ear to a puddle
that's why it's hard for me to relate to you now
because I have a night club named after me
and you are still looking for your Lego's head

SUNDAY I SHOW UP AT AR'S ON IMPULSE

she has the apartment to herself
we debate if we should watch a movie
knowing movie means hooking up
AR leans for movie
AR—only semi-attractive to me
but still attractive
I wonder what she looks like without her sweatshirt
we scroll Netflix but nothing hooks me
every movie looks the same
AR shows me her online journal
my name appears 28 times
I journal on paper (obviously, dear reader)
AR twirls
we eat
we listen to the Beach Boys struggle in the studio
I don't think we can kiss unless we pick a movie
but AR squirms
she kisses well
almost like TK (pre-semester abroad)
or like SN (that one time)
seeing her breasts for the first time, felt relief
to have found out the secret of what kind of nipples
brownish, nice
the Beach Boys studio recordings are filled with unbearable
tension and disappointment

often the track stops
and the main guy explains to the others how he wants it to go
this too happens with AR
but we find our way through
her orgasm is breathy (not at all like TK's!)
and I find that empty apartment and all
I can't fully let loose
I start journaling in my head at moments
like Beach Boys studio comparison—I think that at the time
and instead of saying it
see myself writing in these waiting pages

THE YOGA INSTRUCTOR

she spread oil on the back of my ears and neck
while I relaxed on the mat in *shivasanah*, which must mean rest
or spiritual something

the oil took me from my petty fantasies
and dropped me into a vast, universal fantasy
a way to live beautifully like beasts

horrid sights I'd recently witnessed
flashed and receded
a top hat filled with puke
a woman stuffing dollars into a dog's mouth

as I performed my gawky rendition of the poses
yoga seemed like the quickest, cheapest way to soothe humans

later, an iguana slinked up the steps in a macho, prehistoric way
and the oil wafted from my neck
like I too was an incredible lizard
and not a systems analyst

THE ASSES OF TEENAGERS

the sun warms the asses of teenagers
teenagers have no idea where the day will take them
but we have a pretty good idea
the sun passes over our asses
easily resisting them
across the street, long grass sways in the sun
our asses are freezing in fake denim jeans
and layers upon layers of scratchy discount long johns
teenagers flash their asses outside the movie theater at night
blinding deer and making friends
we just use our asses for sitting
but teenagers are beyond us
wading through a sea of ideas
their boredom is pure and crystalizes
while our boredom stops up the sink
and wears down watch batteries
the sun sees in teenagers something to warm
and pulls them to unpopulated, interesting corners in town
while the unforgiving cold ushers us back
into our cavernous apartments
to sit on our asses and stress about life

EASY VICTORIES

dilly-dallying, I win the race

the dress is given to me without a struggle from the bride

my trophy shelf is featured in *Trophy Weekly*

HE'S GOT A HUGE SOHO LOFT, BUT NO DICK

he's got a really big vocabulary but no dick to speak of
he's got a motorcycle parked in the garage
but still…
he's never had a dick or lost it?
I'm in his loft, like where is it?
he shows me his watch collection
his high thread count
he has a valuable stock portfolio
I left feeling amiss
I called my friend
He's got a great personality but no dick, I said
Front row tickets to the concert, but…
he called and I put my friend on hold
he said, I have something for you
I said, Did I leave my bag?
he said, Yes, you left your bag
but I have something else to show you
and I felt a ripple of life within me
I walked hurriedly back to his loft
Look, he said holding it in his hands
it twisted around his arm
its little tongue felt like sandpaper
It's endangered, he said
It's my brother's, he admitted
it pumped with air

it curled like smoke
I'd never seen anything like it
What is that? I asked
ready for love

THE ZACK RIVER

moves really fast
has both turtles and frogs
sometimes has poop in it
just kidding
it never has trash in it
God loves it
no one ever drowns in it
it's easy going
it's a cool hangout
adults don't get it
play music on the banks and flowers grow
once a cowboy drank from it
once an alien visited it
it won Best River in 2008

THE WORLD OF MANET

can't find the draft of my new poem The World of Manet
that I wrote on the Metro-North last month
after finding and taking art books from a box on the street
in Hastings-on-Hudson
where I adventurously left my car

a couple weird hours with those books
dragging my own little art history with me
feeling super dignified on the train
gazing at forgotten works of genius
while a man yapped on his phone
sitting on them on the sidewalk outside Kathleen's office
so as not to dirty my dress

I left the books in Brooklyn
there was one about Titian too, and another I can't remember
never getting to cull them for phrases like I'd like to
plus can't find the draft, which I scrawled on the back of a poem
I was going to read
and then did read at Berl's

but I know the poem will be good
because the title of the book The World of Manet is so dramatic
and fun to use in a line, like

"I left the world of Manet in Brooklyn!"
like I was carrying it around

but I need to cull the phrases
that made Manet seem like such an amusing badass
a victim of Parisian gossip
and made the old world seem funny and amazing
the details I can't fake now
plus the stuff I wrote on the train
about wanting two statues on either side of my front door
of men covering their crotches
like I saw in the book

I just walked back into the dark hotel room
where John is sleeping
and he asked "who is it?"
as he often asks while he's asleep

I'm so far from The World of Manet
but the idea swells in my mind
and I've brought you all the way here
a bit early to the party
so feel the need to spill my guts
to keep you here longer
because John's asleep
and my world is dim
I haven't seen a good painting in awhile
or made a good painting in longer

if you have the desire to paint
you must paint today
and don't show anyone
be Manet alone
wear a fucking robe
feel those ancient drugs
see the curtain and die a little
Manet was so dashing
painters were so serious
but no one is dashing and serious now

DREAM BOY

I play in the eyes
the eyes are TVs
the eyes look out to the hillside
I flip the channels
I run through the body
I watch the mind spark
I write in my own thoughts
I stroke the brain absentmindedly
I'm gross
covered in tears
blood and whatever else
I sleep in the balls
I struggle up the ribs
I sleep in the mouth
I can't die
I'm a fairy in a boy
I'm listening to the droning of who's talking to him
I can read by the eyes
the eyes let in a little light
I can escape through the ears
but I just beam out
I ball up into fuzz
I burst in the air like dust
I stretch over him like a tight suit
the boy is mortal

can't do anything but live
I grow bored
I dream up his dreams
and press them in
it all feels like maintenance
his friends drone on and on
the fluids! the mucus!
I need to bathe away from beings
I need to spend a summer in the garden
like last summer
but always a dimwit intrigues me
his voice trailing into a bar
I want to see the civilization inside him
never is it as enriching as a book
always he meets a being
a woman from the supermarket
or his own staggering self in the mirror
I should be exploring tombs
like Elsie does
but the smell!
I can't imagine

WHAT I'M GONNA DO TO YOU

first I'm gonna strip you of your stupid clothes
then I'm gonna check my phone for new texts
then I'm gonna look up Pippi Longstocking's Wikipedia page

first I'm gonna get naked
then I'm gonna pace like a security guard
then I'm gonna RSVP to my friend's baby shower
(you don't have to go)

first I'm gonna take your dick in my mouth
then I'm gonna complain about my job at Urban Outfitters

I'm naked and crawling towards you
but I gotta take out recycling
floss
pay Comcast bill
return library book
call my Mom back

let's do it
after I return that picture frame at Target
wash the yams
fix clogged drain in shower

I want you naked and hard
then I'll clean crumbs off the counter

I want you tied to the bedposts
high off dick pills
hungry for pussy
then I'll tell you a funny thing my friend said
and write in this Thank You card to someone's Nanna

IN THE BIBLE I LOVED YOU

it is claustrophobic in the pages
but it was vast in the night

before I dated Ploira I was always over-brushing my horse's mane
thinking of you
carrying hay back to the stable

the sun beat me down
the wind wound me up
the smell of me was never far from me

during the drought I developed a real spot for you
I threw stale bread at my sister
and watched her rip hard crumbs from it

you were sleeping in a field
coated with flies
you would play your harp sometimes
but never did you play for me
you looked at Samuel's cousin with hatred
when he gave me his family's runt of a hen
never did I see gold
but always did I expect to find it
in the shallow graves

Maevid's mane was shiny
mine was full of snarls
I let Samuel's cousin cut it on a rock with a sharp edge
and no one regarded me as a woman
you especially never played your harp for me then
father said I had never looked less like my mother

"Who is that," I asked him finally, "who mopes in the hills?"
but Ploira danced up to me just then
back from her winter mourning

she took my shorn hair in her hands
heat sang out of her
"Let us go to the shack of Forrow's widow"
she whispered
and Samuel's cousin crept away with aversion

TUESDAY

failed History quiz
played dodge-ball
ate pizza bagel
then in Spanish, Mr. Felipé christened me María
he lead me down a flowered path
the air smelt salty like the sea
¿Where is the bibliotheca?
I asked in my most sultry voice
though we both know I hate books

MY HIGH

don't kill my high
it's wimpy, like a tissue
don't rustle it too much
I like it
like a purse
I tuck it here
under my arm
tell me about your weekend
I curl up and listen
your voice waves along
don't tell me too much
limit the parts that don't touch me
those parts get far away like a dreamland
a hell house
really
it cuts us apart
god
you dwindle my high
you don't mean to
but I snap back into myself
my outfit, plain
the usual truth
this evening I'm uneasy
fix me or leave me
I can have fun by myself

I was having it before this
I was loving the world
more than animals love the world
I was feeling the way roads feel
you're always talking about your neighbor
she must have a great body
when you set your attention on things
they shimmer in the light
in the dark of your attention
mushrooms grow around me

be candid with me
carry my mind with a story
or, just like confess something
can you do that?
any little thing
it wouldn't seem little right now
it would occupy me
like the radio
don't leave me for the other things
I know how many other things there are
I see myself, stuck in the fence
I'm with you, yet I still miss you
I can get sort of addicted to talking to you
like now I really have little to say
but feel a real urge to say anything
think of me as a prophet or an angel
someone who gets painted

I need a snack
I get translucent
like no one knows me
this high before
I know, you must go
but it was lamp-like
it rose me up in the tub
my glance had this glaze to it
briefly it chose me
a melody
no, it wasn't like that
lighter than that
I've passed it to you
this temporary joy
you're going to spend it with someone else
roast over it like a meal
part of me is in it
this bundle of light
the gut of your good time
yes
okay
I can barely hear you
it's like you're out in the world
was that a car?
yes, bye
I'm not mad
I'm neutral
I don't have anything to say

I just get to where I like talking
I go in my bed and sink
some feeling grabs like dough and--
yes bye
have fun there
I'll stay here after
listening to the tone
to the town's sleep breathing
to the bugs
yes
bye

I'm here after
alone in the arena
with scraps on the floor
I'm like a shipwrecked explorer
no, a common person
there are pens on the floor
and my underwear in a crumple
I can still find a thought line to you
or better yet, to my ancestors
who see the blinking
I can carry the song through
I won't clear my mind of thoughts
I'll just braid the thoughts
I'll keep holding the rope
it love-lights the dark
I'm getting tired

you are sleeping beside me
hopelessly far
my ancestors meander towards the phone
it takes them awhile
they sense me like bubbles
they are wise and laugh
their laughs are heroic
they are sitting on warm rocks
no
on cushions

I WANNA B A MOUNTAIN

does a mountain still get her period?
I wanna b a racoon
but still date Donny H. like I do now
I see two earths in my eyes in Art Class
in teacher's mirror
if I go to college, I need it to be *Dance College*
where I can major in Sex
I need my future to be E-Z
and lazy
with or without Donny
with good jeans
and no cancers
I'll b a human ATM
and give people cash
I wanna b a lake
but still look great naked
I wanna b a field
and feel when bugs land
I wanna b done with the school day
and eat chocolate in my kitchen
and wonder what's on TV
or why I'm female
I wanna b a cloud
but still text at the beach
that's when texting feels best

that's when I love that boy from camp
that's when I feel modern and quaint
like a cool Amish bitch
I wanna b God's girlfriend
and live on other planets
I wanna break up with God
and watch his wrath
and laugh and laugh

ELIZA KEPT CALLING ME GREAT

I imagined my mind was each minute
making hallways to new parts of the mansion
I saw people as their parents' dreams and troubles
each a piece in the big game
the air felt better than air
I was snug inside my high school poems
that began from a sense of well-being
then danced into a dark spot
a school trip into darkness
and now I'm wondering
what was that earlier thought?
was it just that the past and future are dreams?
and my earlier earlier thought
what was that one?
something damning and exciting about people
about people growing
I can't remember
I've talked too much
to too many people
but I'm proud of how bad my hair must look
and how I'm about to meet up with you as a mind
within a mess
a string of moments clinging together
I have lost my great realization about people
I've just taken a good five minutes to sit and really try to remember

I'm sitting on some church steps if you can believe it
I just farted against them
the air is warm
like it was in high school
and I've made a full circle back to this same block
I just farted again
and it sounded nothing like a fart
but like a plastic toy falling down steps
I leave the churchyard
feeling gothic
like a minor character in a play
(or why not—a major one!)
and walk a block to the school
examining the children's art on display
intrinsically knowing which puppets other puppets would find
sexually attractive
I meet up with you and soon after
a woman with eyes gleaming of infinite possibility
asks for bus money
insisting on how young we look
her shirt is covered in question marks
giving her money feels like the right move in a video game
and we find ourselves at the bad prom sushi place
in a good example of my high without weed feeling
I waltz through the next couple hours
an ATM hangout in the little glass room
a sink in the Ethiopian restaurant bathroom
where the hot water combines with the cold

on a little porcelain piece above the bowl
making me feel like an alchemist
hours later I remember my idea
that people aren't just wanting their lover
to take the place of their mother or father
no
people want their lover
to replace their mother, father, brother, sister, and dog
and no one can do it!
that was the thought
no one is reasonable!
maybe animals are
the people thought isn't as great as I'd remembered
doesn't wow me this time
feels like a thought almost everyone thought today
but I have great instincts!
Eliza said
though she is high off new love and her finished screenplay
and I want to write of the bathroom line drama
the butt foam
why my heart was pounding in the bookstore
we pass hell-storm Brooklyn
and I look at plastic bags
among the chain-link
like caught souls
eventually, my vivacity is overpowered by cruel internet bloopers
shitload of pain
and the familiar boredom

that finds us all
that nestles up
that sets right down
but the past is a story
and the future a less detailed story
and the dream sticks a little on both ends

KITCHENS IN THE MIDDLE OF THE NIGHT

never turn the light on
in the kitchen at night
don't disrupt the order
the waiting
and longing
I walk into my kitchen and end up in yours
only in the middle of the night
when nothing knows my name
one can love anyone in the kitchen at night
the heart beats slower
the dishes quiet in drawers
the dim crumbs
black windows
that light footstep of yours
lovers linger in the kitchen of their lover
hungry after midnight
searching for their phone
kitchens tolerate human searching
exquisite security in the kitchen at night
forgotten by all
but still flickering
between worlds like a smoke curl
as the earth inches along

a planet filled with kitchens
people do terrible things far from the sun
but you cannot do anything that terrible

MY NAKED PRINCESS

you have the right face for everything
except charity work
except zookeeper

I WANT TO LISTEN TO SHANE AND NORA MAKE LOVE

let's schedule around that
let's listen to the breath escape in short sniffs and gasps
I can't hear the bed
can you hear the bed?
I can't feel the hot skin
I can almost feel the hot skin
can they hear us through the door?
are they thinking of us like we are thinking of them?
are they thinking at all?
is there hair?
is it good?
it sounds good
I want to be wrapped in sheets
instead of standing here holding this umbrella
how old are they anyway?
they seem young
they aren't lying
they are trying so hard to be quiet
or their sex is just quiet
is he in her?
what are their mouths doing?
how are they situated?
I like to lose my mind in sex
are you into sex?
do you talk during sex?

I like to lose my name and my life in sex
I like to float around the room
I like how Nora doesn't wear make-up
I will stop wearing make-up
and I like how confidently Shane pitched his movie before
I should pitch my movie like that
I like this time of year
cracking the ice with my boots
going to new restaurants
it sounds like they have stopped
or it's too muffled
I like how it sounds
the rush of sex
melts the clock
I think I can hear it again
Shane and Nora
those religious sounds of asking

Earlier versions of these poems previously appeared in *Two Serious Ladies*, *jubilat*, *PEN Poetry*, *iO*, *Hobart*, *Everyday Genius*, *Atlas Review*, *The Fiddleback*, *Pleiades*, *Similar Peaks*, *Pop Serial*, *Western Beefs of North America*, and *Poetry & Criticism* (a Korean Anthology).

Special thanks to Karen & Jerry Glaser, Dan Glaser, John Maradik, Ben Estes, Alan Felsenthal, Ryan MacDonald, Mary Austin Speaker, Factory Hollow Press, Flying Object, Lauren Sphorer and *Two Serious Ladies*, Mojo Lorwin, Max Bean, Jack Christian, Seth Landman, Ted Powers, Peter Gizzi, Dara Wier, Sandy Florian, Joana Howard, Mairead Byrne, Lynn Bailey, Karen Rile, Claudia Ballard, GRANTA, The Gorgeous Hen, AC, AK, BB, CC, CD, C.S., DC, DB, EP, ES, GP, HC, HT, JSK, JV, LB, LY, ML, Mf, MY, MT, NO, my jersey crew, RISD friends, The Maradiks, The Millay Colony, and Buck's Rock.

OTHER TITLES FROM THE SONG CAVE: